P R E D A T O R S
VULTURES

Jinny Johnson

Belitha Press

LOOK FOR THE PREDATOR
Look for the vulture in boxes like this.
Here you will find extra facts, stories
and other interesting information about vultures.

First published in the UK in 2003 by

Belitha Press
A member of **Chrysalis** Books plc
64 Brewery Road, London N7 9NT

Design and editorial production
Bender Richardson White
Copyright © Belitha Press 2002

ISBN 1 84138 671 5

British Library Cataloguing in Publication Data for this book is available from the British Library.

10 9 8 7 6 5 4 3 2 1

J159,184
£17·00

▼ **An African white-backed vulture on a branch, looking out for a possible meal (see page 7).**

Acknowledgements
We wish to thank the following individuals and organizations for their help and assistance and for supplying material in their collections:
CORBIS Corporation/Images: pages 1, 4; 11 top, 20 (Papilio); 14 (D. Robert & Lorri Franz); 23 bottom (Eric & David Hosking); 26 (Bettman); 27 (Gianni Dagli Orti). Gallo Images: pages 2, 7 bottom (Peter Lillie); 3, 19 top, 19 bottom (Anthony Bannister Photo Library); 12 (Keith Begg/Anthony Bannister Photo Library); 15 (Martin Harvey); 21 top (Nigel Dennis/Anthony Bannister Photo Library); 28 (Eric Reisinger/Anthony Bannister Photo Library); 30 (Richard du Toit). Frank Lane Photo Agency: pages 5 top, 13 top, 29 (Fritz Polking); 5 bottom, 17 bottom (T. DeRoy/Minden Pictures); 7 top (Gerard Lacz); 8 top, 11 bottom, 14-15, 3 (E & D Hosking); 13 bottom (Philip Perry); 16 (Jurgen & Christine Sohns); 17 top (W. S. Clark). Natural History Photo Agency: pages 6, 18 (Nigel J. Dennis); 8 bottom (Jany Sauvanet); 9 (Eckart Pott); 10 (Rich Kirchner); 21 bottom, 24 (Daniel Heuclin); 22 (Daryl Balfour), 23 top (Julie Meech), 25 top (John Hartley), 25 bottom (Roger Tidman).
Front and back covers: Frank Lane Photo Agency (Fritz Polking).
Back cover: ECOSCENE (Michael Gore).

Editorial Manager: Joyce Bentley
Assistant Editor: Clare Chambers
Project Editor: Lionel Bender
Text Editor: Kate Phelps
Design and Make-up: Ben White
Picture Research: Cathy Stastny
Consultant: John Stidworthy

Printed in Hong Kong

CONTENTS

▶ White-headed vultures
pick on bones
(see page 19).

AMAZING SCAVENGERS

A vulture is a type of bird. Like all birds, a vulture has feathers, wings to power its flight and it lays eggs. There are two groups of vultures: Old World and New World. Old World vultures live in southern Europe, Africa and Asia. They are related to eagles, hawks and falcons. New World vultures live in North and South America. They may be related to storks.

▼ A vulture sits on a branch high above the ground where it can look for carrion.

There are 15 species, or types, of Old World vulture and seven types of New World vulture. Most are large birds, but species range in weight from less than 1 kg to about 14 kg. Vultures can fly long distances as they search the land for food to eat. Condors, which belong to the New World vulture group, are some of the largest of all flying birds.

LITTLE VOICE

New World vultures and condors do make some noises, such as grunts and coughs, but they do not make sounds like other birds. They do not have a syrinx – an organ like our voice box – that produces sound and song in most birds.

▲ A group of White-backed vultures peck hungrily at a carcass as more birds fly down to join them. White-backed vultures live in southern Africa.

With their hooked beaks, broad wings and large feet, vultures look like fierce predators, or hunters. Most predators kill other animals to eat. These animals are called their prey. Vultures do kill some prey, but they get most of their food by scavenging. This means that they feed mainly on the bodies of animals that are already dead. This dead and rotting flesh is called carrion.

▶ The Andean condor is the largest of the New World vultures, with a wingspan of more than 3 m. The male is slightly bigger than the female, and he has a fleshy wattle on his head.

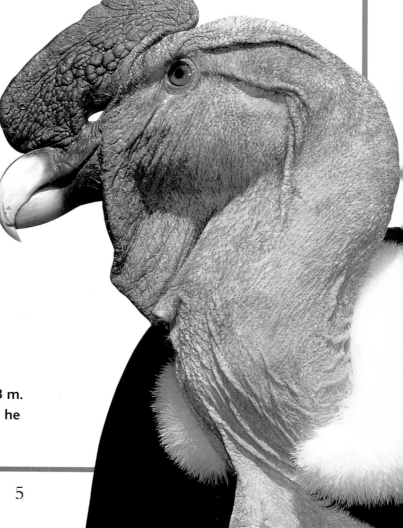

KILLING MACHINE

Vultures are powerful birds, perfectly equipped for their hunting and scavenging lifestyle. They have long broad wings that allow them to soar for hours as they search for prey. Their eyesight is excellent.

The beak is large and hooked for tearing flesh out of carcasses. However, not all vultures have a beak strong enough to cut through tough mammal skin. If carrion is scarce, most vultures will kill their own prey. When times are hard, they will even eat insects and other small creatures.

BIG BIRD

The name vulture comes from a Latin word *vellere*, which means 'to tear at'. The bird probably got this name because of the way it tears and rips at carcasses as it feeds. The name condor comes from an Inca word that means simply 'big bird'.

◀ Lammergeiers live in parts of southern Europe, Asia and Africa. They have a wingspan of more than 2.5 m and weigh up to 7 kg.

◀ The scramble at a carcass is not as chaotic as it looks. Different types of vulture feed on different parts of the body.

Most vultures have a bare head with only a thin covering of down. This is ideal for a bird that has such a messy way of feeding. A vulture with a feathered head would have a lot of cleaning to do after plunging its beak deep into a carcass. The bare head may also help to keep the vulture cool during hot weather. Many vultures do have a ruff of feathers around the neck that helps keep them warm at night when temperatures fall.

▼ African white-backed vultures may gather in groups of 100 or more birds at one carcass.

WHERE VULTURES LIVE

Vultures live across much of the world – North and South America, Africa, Asia and southern Europe – in a range of different habitats. There are no vultures in Australia or New Zealand.

In the Americas, the Andean condor flies over the rugged landscape of the Andes Mountains, where it nests on mountain ledges. In contrast, the Turkey vulture hunts for food in dense forests, although it also flies over grassland. The Black vulture is common in towns and villages, where it boldly scavenges on waste in markets, backyards and harbours. The Turkey vulture lives farther north than any other vulture and, during summer, is even seen in Canada. In winter, it flies south to escape the cold.

▲ With a wingspan of over 3 m, the European black vulture is the largest of the Old World vultures, but it is now very rare.

► A flock of American black vultures scavenge for fish waste and other refuse in a harbour. These vultures have learned that food is plentiful wherever humans live.

▶ The Lappet-faced vulture of Africa is usually seen in savanna and dry scrubland, where it often roosts high in acacia trees.

In Africa and Asia, vultures are commonly found in savanna and scrubland areas where carrion is easy to spot. Hooded vultures and Egyptian vultures are often seen in towns, and they also follow herds of livestock to snatch scraps to eat. Roadkills of pets and wild animals are another good source of food for these birds. These ready-made meals have helped vultures survive and even increase in numbers when other predators are becoming rare.

GIANT RELATIVE

The first vultures lived millions of years ago. Fossils have been found of a giant relative of New World vultures that lived in Argentina between 20 and 5 million years ago. This bird, called *Argentavis*, was 1.5 m tall and had wings that measured more than 7 m from tip to tip.

VULTURE FOOD

Carrion is the main food of vultures. Some species also kill prey and steal eggs, and the Egyptian vulture eats plant material as well as meat. The Lappet-faced vulture – the largest vulture in Africa – hunts both adult and young flamingos and may also kill young gazelles and small mammals such as hares.

Like other vultures, the Egyptian vulture takes carrion when it can find it, but will also gobble up rotting fruit and vegetables and any small insects and lizards it can catch. It also eats eggs and is among the very few birds to use tools in its efforts to feed.

If an egg is small enough, the vulture picks it up and smashes it against a rock or the ground to break it open. But an ostrich egg is too large for the bird to hold in its beak. Instead, it picks up a heavy stone and hurls it at the egg until the shell cracks and releases its nourishing contents for the bird to lap up.

▼ Turkey vultures often live in built-up areas and have learned to take advantage of creatures killed on the road, like this snake.

► The tool-using habit of the Egyptian vulture is not instinctive. This very intelligent bird learns how to break eggs open by watching other Egyptian vultures at work.

BONE BREAKER

In order not to waste any food, the lammergeier will even feed on bones. Its tongue has special grooves for removing the marrow from bones. To break the bone into pieces it can swallow, the lammergeier carries them high into the air and drops them on to a rock where they smash and splinter. The bird then swallows pieces of bone whole. The bones are broken down by its powerful digestive juices.

Strangest of all is the Palm-nut vulture, an African bird that feeds on the fruit of the oil palm. The vulture hangs upside-down in the tree and, having plucked a fruit, holds it in its feet while it pulls off the flesh. Some experts believe, however, that this bird is not a vulture but a fish eagle.

◄ Ruppell's griffon vulture can go for days without food. When it does find a carcass, it may eat as much as 1.5 kg of meat at one sitting – making it too heavy to fly again for a few hours!

FIERCE WEAPONS

A vulture's main weapon is its hooked beak, which it uses to feed on carrion or sometimes to kill live prey. Birds such as the Lappet-faced vulture in Africa and the King vulture in South America have beaks that are strong enough to pierce the tough skin of large mammals. These vultures are also helped by their large size. Other scavengers give way when they arrive at a carcass.

Smaller vultures with weaker beaks depend on their relatives to open up a carcass so that everyone can get to the feast. The Hooded and Egyptian vultures, for example, have longer, thinner beaks than other vultures, ideal for snapping up titbits. They also catch insects and small creatures such as lizards.

▼ This White-backed vulture's strong tongue is clearly visible here. Its rough, rasping surface helps the bird remove flesh from bone.

▶ One of the strongest of all vultures, the Lappet-faced vulture rips open a carcass with its beak.

Other birds of prey, such as eagles and hawks, use their feet and long, curving talons for killing prey. But a vulture's feet are shaped more for walking and running and are little use as weapons. Most vultures, except the lammergeier, cannot even carry food in their feet.

▲ Like most vultures, the Himalayan griffon has large feet with hooked talons, but these are weak compared to those of other birds of prey.

SICK TRICK

Vultures do not have many enemies, but if the Turkey vulture does want to defend itself from danger, it vomits on its attacker. The bird can project its vomit nearly 2 m. And when its enemy has gone, the vulture eats the vomit again so as not to waste good food!

VULTURE SENSES

For Old World vultures, keen eyesight is their most important sense when searching for prey. They circle high above the land until they spot a likely meal on the ground. Their good sight also helps vultures keep an eye on each other – if one is seen landing, others suspect it has found food and are quick to follow. Condors, too, have good sight and can spot a carcass from a great distance.

Unlike most birds, the American turkey vulture has a powerful sense of smell. Its nostrils are larger than those of other vultures, and the part of its brain that deals with smell is bigger too. Its ability to sniff out a meal means that it can find food in dense forest that may not be seen from the air.

▶ Vultures' keen sight allows them to see prey from high above the ground.

◀ The Turkey vulture's sense of smell is thought to be at least three times more powerful than that of other New World vultures.

SHARP EYESIGHT

The eyes of a bird of prey such as a vulture are large for the bird's size and can point both forwards and sideways. The strongly curved cornea admits plenty of light to the eye, and a large number of light-sensitive cells allow very precise vision. Experts think that vultures can spot a metre-long carcass from more than 6 km away in open country.

▲ The King vulture has a poor sense of smell and relies on following smaller vultures to find food.

Other vultures with less keen noses watch the movements of the Turkey vulture carefully and soon join it. Even though it has to share its meal, the Turkey vulture benefits from the arrival of its stronger-beaked relatives – they can tear open the carcass so everyone can feed. The Turkey vulture's relatives, the Yellow-headed vultures of North and South America, also have a good sense of smell.

HIGH FLIERS

Vultures are a magnificent sight as they soar high above the ground on broad outstretched wings. In the right conditions they hardly need to move their wings; they simply glide on air currents.

Gliding is vital to vultures' success because they may have to fly long distances in order to find enough food to eat. In many places, the birds use thermals – currents of warm air that rise from the land below during the day. The vultures hitch a ride on the thermals and can float for hours. In its mountain home, the Andean condor soars on air forced up by high ground. It is believed to reach heights of more than 11 000 m above sea level. When landing, a vulture lowers its legs and spreads out its feet. They act as brakes as the vulture touches the ground.

AIR ACE

The Griffon vulture is superb in the air. It can fly for 6 or 7 hours at 50 km/h without a break and is often seen at heights of more than 3300 m. It has been known to fly as high as 9000 m. When a meal is in sight, it can dive to the ground at speeds of up to 160 km/h.

▶ One of North America's largest birds of prey, the Turkey vulture, is 80 cm long and its wingspan measures 1.8 m.

Like most vultures, the Griffon vulture has very widely spaced primary feathers that may help to increase lift when the bird is in the air. The bird opens or closes its wings slightly to adjust the amount of lift.

The Andean condor is known to fly up to heights of 5000 m. Although its wings are slightly shorter than those of the Wandering albatross, they are broader so the condor's wing area is the largest of any bird.

Vultures are heavy for their size but their weight helps them keep a steady course when gliding at high speeds. Much of their weight is a store of fat that they use for energy. With this store, they don't have to eat every day.

GOING HUNTING

For a vulture, hunting depends as much on checking what other vultures are up to as finding prey for itself. Once a carcass is spotted the vultures are quick to drop to the ground, one after the other.

On the African grasslands, the first to arrive is often a smaller type such as the White-headed vulture. It can peck at the soft parts of a carcass but depends on the larger vultures to open up the body. Next may come the griffons, which tend to live in colonies and gather at a carcass in large numbers. Finally, the Lappet-faced vulture, largest of the African vultures, may arrive. The strongest of all with a powerful beak, this vulture can tear open the tough skin of an elephant or zebra.

◄ Competition at a carcass can be fierce and squabbles do break out over tasty morsels. Less than an hour after an animal dies, it may already be surrounded by 200 or more vultures.

▶ White-backed vultures do not usually dig deep into carcasses but pick up the scraps left by other birds. They also catch insects and stranded fish.

Vultures do not rely on finding the leftovers from large predators such as lions. More of their food comes from old or sick animals that have died naturally from age, illness or hunger, and from stillborn or injured young. In the breeding season, male vultures fly back to their nests after feeding and regurgitate food for their mates and young.

▼ These White-headed vultures have stripped this zebra carcass in the African savanna.

BIG LUNCH

Vultures are hearty eaters and when they find a good meal, they will eat as much as they can. A vulture may eat up to a quarter of its own body weight at one time, but such a meal can last it for weeks.

PICKING BONES

Most vultures feed entirely on meat, but they aren't fussy eaters. When a vulture feeds, it holds on to the carcass with its feet and uses its beak to pull flesh off the bones. Some birds also delve deep inside the body and every bit is used.

White-backed vultures, for example, eat mostly the soft flesh, while Lappet-faced vultures seem to prefer skin and tendon. Griffon vultures feast on muscle and internal organs. The smaller species such as Hooded vultures and Egyptian vultures gobble up the scraps dropped by larger birds and peck marrow from splintered bones. Some vultures prefer fresh carrion, but others will feed on rotting meat without any harm to themselves.

▼ Larger birds may drive their smaller, weaker relatives away from a carcass.

▼ The largest flying bird in North America, the California condor, can eat up to a kilogram of food a day.

The birds feed so efficiently that after half an hour or so of feeding on a carcass, only the bones are left. They don't need to drink much since they get moisture from their food.

AIR CONDITIONING

Vultures have a strange way of keeping cool in hot weather – they squirt their urine over their legs. As the urine evaporates, it cools the bird. The vulture's bare head also helps to keep its body cool.

21

NATURE'S CLEANERS

Thousands of animals die each year in areas such as the African savanna, but thanks to vultures their bodies are quickly and easily disposed of. Without vultures, more animal carcasses would be left to rot and could spread disease.

▼ African white-backed vultures on an elephant carcass.

GRISLY END

Vultures have been known to flock to battlegrounds to feed on the dead. After the Charge of the Light Brigade in the Crimean War in 1854, soldiers had to patrol the battlefield, shooting vultures in order to protect the wounded.

The birds themselves don't seem to come to any harm from their grisly feeding habits. Their bare heads ensure that they don't have to spend time preening head feathers soaked with blood after a meal. And any harmful bacteria on the meat seem to be killed by the strong acids in the vulture's digestive system.

After feeding, vultures usually bask in the sun for a while. Any bits of blood and meat that have stuck to their feathers then dry and fall off or are removed when the bird preens itself.

▼ Hooded vultures will take any food they can get, including turtles and shellfish on the seashore.

▼ Vultures at a water hole. These birds produce urine that contains very little water so they do not need to drink very often.

UNDER THREAT

Some kinds of vulture are now very rare. Birds have long been shot as pests and poisoned by the chemicals, such as pesticides, used on farmland.

Changes in farming methods have caused problems, and in some areas it is hard for vultures to find food – dead animals are removed from the land too quickly nowadays. Also in some countries the vultures' usual habitat has been destroyed – grassland and scrub have become towns and cities, and so there are fewer wild animals to feed on.

Some vultures, such as the Black vulture, have managed to adapt, and they now find food more easily around towns and cities than on grassland. Roadkills also provide food for urban vultures. Large vultures, such as the condors, now only survive because they are protected.

▼ California condors have bred successfully in San Diego Zoo, and the species has been rescued from extinction.

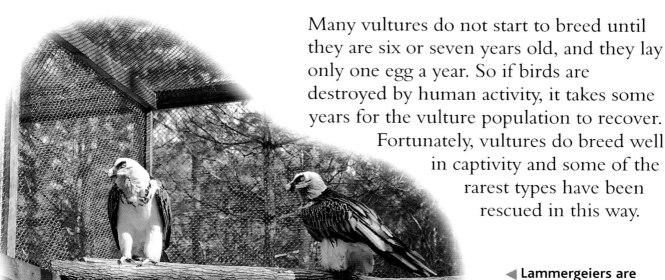

Many vultures do not start to breed until they are six or seven years old, and they lay only one egg a year. So if birds are destroyed by human activity, it takes some years for the vulture population to recover. Fortunately, vultures do breed well in captivity and some of the rarest types have been rescued in this way.

◀ Lammergeiers are among the rarest of all European birds of prey. They, too, are being reared in breeding centres and then put back into the wild.

BREEDING SUCCESS

During the twentieth century, the California condor became so rare that by 1985 there were only nine known birds left. It was decided to capture these condors and keep them at two zoos in California so that more birds could be bred in safety. This has been a success, and since 1992 condors have been released back into the wild.

▶ Numbers of Griffon vultures are low, and birds bred in captivity have been released in Europe.

VULTURE FACTS

Vultures were once believed to have special magical powers. They have featured in the myths and legends of many countries for thousands of years.

SACRED SITES

In ancient Egypt, the mother goddess, Mut, was shown with a vulture's head or with a vulture for a crown. The vulture was also sacred to the goddess Nekhbet, who was a protector of the pharaoh, ruler of Egypt. Nekhbet appears in paintings with a vulture's head, and her vulture adorns the pharaoh's crown. Precious objects bearing pictures of vultures were often placed in tombs to provide protection for the person in the next life.

CONDOR POWER

For North American Indians, the condor was a symbol of power. They used condor feathers and even live condors in their dances and ceremonies.

THUNDER GOD

Alaskan Indians believed the California condor to be a thunder god who created storms.

◀ **One of the treasures found in the tomb of Tutankhamen, the ancient Egyptian pharaoh, was a magnificent collar. This was in the shape of a vulture with widespread wings. It was made of gold, precious stones and coloured glass.**

MESSENGER OF THE GODS

The Incas of Peru believed that the condor was a messenger from the sun god, and pictures of the condor appeared on pots, jewellery and other items. One ancient story relates how every morning the condor lifts the sun high into the sky and later returns it to a lake for the night. Today, some South American Indians still believe that illnesses can be cured by eating the powdered bones or dried heart of a condor and that swallowing a condor's eye improves eyesight.

SCAVENGER BIRD

The Iroquois people of North America have a legend that explains how the vulture became a scavenger. When all the birds were given jobs by the Golden Eagle, king of the birds, the vulture was told to clean up carrion and continues to do so to the present day.

FORTUNE TELLERS

In Africa, it is a traditional belief of the Shona tribe that vultures can foretell the future, because they seem always able to find food. The Shona mix the ground heart of a White-backed vulture with certain plants and use it with divining bones when predicting events in the future.

▲ The Nazca Indians lived in Peru more than 1000 years ago. They, like the Incas, often used condor images on their pottery.

DEADLY MISTAKE

An ancient Greek story tells of a lammergeier that was flying by with a tortoise it had just found to eat. The bird looked down and saw what it thought was a rock. It dropped the tortoise to smash it open and make it easy to eat. Unfortunately what the lammergeier saw was not a rock but the bald head of the famed poet Aeschylus, who was killed by the falling tortoise.

VULTURE WORDS

This glossary explains some of the words used in this book that you might not have seen before.

Bacteria
tiny organisms that can cause disease.

Captivity
keeping birds in safety in a zoo or wildlife park while they lay their eggs and rear their young.

Carcass
the dead body of an animal.

Carrion
the flesh of animals that have died naturally or been killed by predators.

Colonies
groups of birds or other creatures which live close together.

Cornea
the curved, transparent area that covers the front of the eye.

Down
small, very soft feathers on the body of a bird.

Extinction
the death of every single member of a species of plant or animal so that the species completely disappears from the Earth.

Fossil
the bones or teeth of a long-dead animal that have become preserved in rock.

Gliding
a bird's method of flying by using lift from natural air currents instead of constantly flapping its wings.

Habitat
the place where an animal or plant lives – for example, savanna or rainforest.

Marrow
the fatty substance in the centre of a bone.

▶ Some mammals are scavengers too, and vultures sometimes have to compete with creatures such as hyenas at a carcass.

New World

the continents of North America and South America.

Old World

the continents of Europe, Africa, Asia and Australia.

Pesticides

chemicals used to destroy weeds, certain insects and other creatures that may damage crops or farmland.

Predator

an animal that hunts other animals and eats them.

Prey

an animal that is killed by another animal for food.

Primary feathers

the large feathers on a bird's wings that allow it to fly.

Regurgitate

to cough up food that is only partly digested, in birds usually to feed young.

Roost

the place, often a tree, where a bird rests or sleeps. When a bird is resting it is said to be roosting.

Savanna

grassland in tropical areas, where there are dry seasons and rainy seasons.

Scavenging

feeding on the dead bodies of animals and other waste matter.

Scrubland

dry land with few plants other than small trees and bushes.

Species

a particular type of animal. The Andean condor is a species of vulture. There are about 22 different species of vulture.

Talons

the hooked claws on a bird's feet.

Water hole

a pool of water to which animals come to drink, especially during the dry season.

Wattle

a loose fold of flesh on the head or neck of a bird.

Wingspan

the measurement from tip to tip of a bird's wings when they are fully spread.

▼ The Andean condor is mostly black with some white on its wings and a ruff of white feathers around its neck. The male has fleshy wattle on his head and brown eyes. Female Andean condors have bright-red eyes.

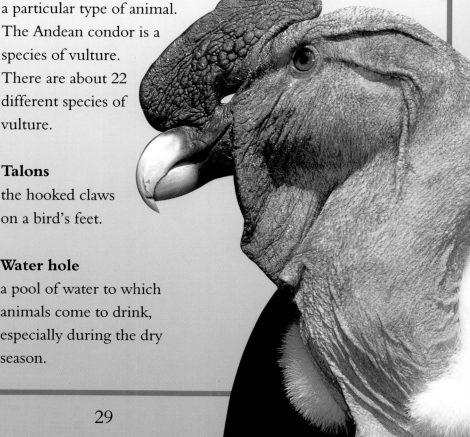

VULTURE PROJECTS

If you want to find out more about vultures, here are some ideas for projects.

WATCHING VULTURES

While you may not be able to watch vultures in the wild, you can often see them in zoos, nature reserves or wildlife parks. Note their bare heads and look at their beaks and feet. There are many other birds that have similar adaptations to scavenging, hunting and catching prey. Make a chart of those you can see: where do these birds live, what do they prey on, and what size are they, their feet and beak compared to the vultures?

WHAT EATS WHAT?

Starting with vultures, draw a food chain of wildlife on the grasslands of Africa. A food chain is a diagram linking each animal with the animals or plants it feeds on. The text in this book will give you some of the 'links' in the chain. Look at the Internet sites opposite to find other links.

▼ The African white-backed vulture has mostly brownish feathers with some white on its lower back. Its wings are dark with white on the underside.

HOW YOU CAN HELP

If you are visiting an area where vultures live and come across any roadkills, don't always be so quick to remove these dead bodies – it may be a meal for a hungry vulture.

Another way to help is to join a conservation group to find out more about vultures and see how you can help them survive in the future. At a zoo or wildlife park, you may be able to adopt a vulture and help to pay for its upkeep.

VULTURES ON THE WEB

If you have access to the Internet, try looking up these websites:

www.vultures.homestead.com
Good general information about Old World and New World vultures.

www.seaworld.org/AnimalBytes/ abvultures.htm
Key facts on vultures.

www.geobop.com/Birds/Falconiformes/ Accipitridae/Vultures/index.htm
Information on the vulture groups and on individual species of vulture.

www.restafrica.org
An organization for the protection of rare and endangered species, with special emphasis on the Cape griffon vulture.

www.peregrinefund.org/conserv_cacondor. html
A website about the breeding programme to save the California condor from extinction.

▼ **A row of vultures on a wildebeest carcass. From left to right: the White-headed vulture, Hooded vulture and White-backed vulture.**

31

INDEX